WE HEARD THE BIRD SING

INTERACTING WITH
ANTHONY DE MELLO, S.J.

COMPILED BY
AUREL BRYS, S.J., AND JOSEPH PULICKAL, S.J.

WE HEARD
THE
BIRD SING

Loyola
Press
Chicago

© 1995 Gujarat Sahitya Prakash, Anand, India
Original English edition

Loyola Press
3441 North Ashland Avenue
Chicago, IL 60657
Phone: (800) 621-1008
FAX: (312) 281-0555

Cover design by Frederick Falkenberg.
Cover art by Bob Masheris.
Interior design by Tammi Longsjo.

Library of Congress Cataloging-in-Publication Data
We heard the bird sing : interacting with Anthony de Mello, S.J. /
    compiled by Aurel Brys and Joseph Pulickal.
        p.   cm.
    ISBN 0-8294-0866-5 (alk. paper)
    1. De Mello, Anthony, 1931–   . 2. Jesuits—India—Biography.
I. Brys, Aurel.   II. Pulickal, Joseph.
BX4705.D2845W4   1995
271'.5302—dc20
    [B]   95-24093
                                                      CIP

A NOTE FROM THE AMERICAN PUBLISHER

Back in 1992 and 1993 we published Tony de Mello's last posthumous publication, *One Minute Nonsense,* in two volumes. Then late in 1993 came word from Father X. Diaz del Rio, S.J., director of Gujarat Sahitya Prakash, the original publisher in India, that Father de Mello's mission was still ongoing in a book to come. Father del Rio wrote, "We have another manuscript entitled *We Heard the Bird Sing: Interacting with Anthony de Mello, S.J.* It is a compilation of anecdotes about or what happened with Tony by people who were very close to him. The accounts have been gathered by two Jesuits, close friends of Tony, who had also followed his courses: Father Aurel Brys, a Belgian from Ranchi Jesuit Province, and Father J. Pulickal, a former provincial of Kerala Jesuit Province (India)."

The original publication of *We Heard the Bird Sing*—its title referring to Tony's earlier work *The Song of the Bird*—came early in 1995. But the 1993 notice from Father del Rio attracted attention around the world and led publishers in a number of languages to ask for publishing rights as soon as they became available. We feel fortunate in having secured the rights for the United States and Canada and for putting these exceptional materials in readers' hands a few months later.

In their comments, editors Fathers Pulickal and Brys tell how the idea came for *We Heard the Bird Sing.* As more than one hundred contributors, all of whom had known Tony personally, responded to the compilers' invitation, the editors remark how the anecdotes and stories became, in short order, "a dam-burst of affection and gratitude and esteem" for their mentor and friend. The accounts are presented without titles and, outside of some grouping according to themes, may well stand on their own. At the same time, a kind of video of Tony emerges—arranged according to the compilers' perceptions of the flow of his charismatic life and mission.

Rev. Joseph F. Downey, S.J.
Editorial Director, Loyola Press

PREFACE

I was nervous as I walked into the dining room where Tony and about twenty others were at supper. Later Tony said he did not notice the nervousness but had felt good at seeing me. Strange, I thought.

That was our first meeting.

In Sadhana, 1976–77, I had plenty of personal problems to "solve"—so much so when no one else had anything to say they would tease me: Joe, come out with a problem! And I would, every time! As if that was not enough I also had problems with Tony: his theories, ways. With all that a fond relationship developed between him and me.

It seemed to me he looked forward to the discussions— serious theoretical discussions—we were having after the sessions and whenever we met later.

The difficulties and the affection between us continued till the end. I was uncomfortable about the difficulties; he seemed to forget each unpleasant incident as soon as it was over.

Tony saw in me the good I myself did not see; the bad I was bothered about did not bother him.

When he died I wished very much I could do something "for" him. But what? Gradually the wish faded. Then unexpectedly in March 1992 the idea of the present book occurred to me. I sounded it out with Aurel Brys, Leela Kottoor, and Isabel Martin. It clicked with them. Aurel and I started working.

Some time later I told Aurel: I am one who would wait for the wind to weigh anchor; you would say: if there is no wind, we will row, we will push! But for his rowing and pushing, the idea of the book would have remained an idea!

J. Pulickal, S.J.

Going through the contributions of those who responded to our letter requesting them to write on how Tony had touched and changed their lives, I felt I was on "sacred ground." Their contributions narrated how Tony's interactions had helped and challenged them, had started a process and a movement in them, quickened the pace and enhanced the quality of their lives. These personal stories took me within myself where I met Tony in a new way.

I encountered the spirit of Tony alive in those people, active in that freeing process experienced by them over the years and in their continued search to respond to life's experiences here and now, present in their own desire to respond in new, compassionate ways to their call, at work in the spiritual renewal that Tony had set in motion in India.

While working with Joe on the personal testimonies, something deeper happened. I came to realize how the Gospels must have come about in a similar manner. Editing the various testimonies, the writers did not try to recreate the person of Jesus, but they sought to capture his Spirit.

Discovering and receiving the spirit of Tony has helped me to receive anew the Spirit of Life, the Spirit of Jesus. The magic of Tony had worked once again.

A. Brys, S.J.

INTRODUCTION

What is this book? Our first letter about it, dated April 4, 1992, inviting contributions explained:

> Would you like to contribute to a book on Tony de Mello's work?
>
> If Tony has touched and changed the lives of so many in so many places throughout his ministry, it must be because some things in him were of lasting value and he expressed them with freshness and force. To recapture something of that is our desire.
>
> Do you remember experiencing the "magic" of Tony? in a piece of counseling, spiritual direction, therapy? In an encounter, interaction, theoretical exposition, relationship? In a repartee, story, or joke which drove home a point? If you do, then that is material for our book.
>
> Tony's own books are mostly "anecdotal": collections of stories, exercises, insights, jokes. The proposed book on Tony also will be that: anecdotal. A return of the compliment!
>
> The purpose of the book will not be to show how great Tony was. It is not meant as a tribute to a hero. Pieces merely to satisfy curiosity or to evoke admiration or to give biographical tidbits are not expected.
>
> Your contributions should be narratives of occasions with Tony which challenged you, energized you, opened a window to you, deepened your understanding, made you hear the song of the bird, led you into silence. These must lead the reader to a similar experience.

As the contributions came in, we realized that it would be an impossible task to cleanse them of "tributes to a hero" and of sentiments: what we saw in them was a dam-burst of affection and gratitude and esteem. . . .

All the contributors wrote to us: "do whatever you want with the write-up—correct, recast, shorten, lengthen, reject." We have done all that—we had to! In the process we may have here and there overlooked or misinterpreted the ideas of the writers. But we have been at pains not to do that.

Our perception of the flow of Tony's life has guided us in the ordering of the materials in this book. Within that very loose framework, pieces which deal with the same or similar themes have been grouped. The chronology of Tony's life or of the interactions reported have not been adhered to.

We present the pieces without titles. May each one impress you as would the beauty of an unnamed solitary flower, bird, animal, vista, star, or human scene. We missed Tony's jokes in the write-ups sent to us for the book. What is Tony de Mello without jokes? A man who, in the words of one of our writers, was "a revered-retreat-master and became the irreverent-director-of-Sadhana," and who, in his own words, wanted "to die cracking a joke"! And so we have thrown in a few—they are not his, but taken from other sources. We hope they have something of the two-edged humor and the wisdom-thrust of the typical Tony jokes.

At the end of the book is a section we have entitled ". . . So Happy, So Free. . . ." It contains information on Tony excerpted verbatim from material sent to us. Reviewers of Tony's books have observed that Tony the man remained mysterious to the last. These pieces perhaps reveal the man a little more. Perhaps our entire book does that.

We sent our first letter to about 120 people who had known Tony personally. We could have sent it to 500 if then we had the complete list of those who have done Sadhana— which we now have. That would have made the book richer.

And so this book is not a complete video of Tony at work. To present a comprehensive synthesis of his ideas was never our aim. And we do not analyze or evaluate him. However we want to say this: Tony did not, especially in his later years, represent the mainline Christian thought or piety; but he offered a witness and a program, and raised some questions, which even mainline Christians found immensly challenging and enriching; that was, is, his relevance.

The names of the contributors are printed in alphabetical order (according to first name). Obviously some have written more than one piece. All the names in the interactions are fictitious. The readers would not know who wrote which piece. Thanks to the writers who trusted us with some very personal experiences.

Thanks to the friends who so readily gave us the help we needed: James Pathippallil, John Vattanky, Francis D'Sa, Shanti, Leela, Lisbert, J. Thayil, Isabel, Michael, P. J. Francis, Lucien Clarijsse, Alex Toppo. And thanks to Gujarat Sahitya Prakash.

CONTRIBUTORS

Abe Puthumana, Aurel Brys, Bernadette, Bob Grib, Carlos Valles, Celine, Celene K., C. P. Varkey, Cyriac Muppathy, Delphine, Dina Guha, Dominic George, Estela Cordeiro, Francisca, Frank Stroud, George Ribas, Grace de Mello, Isabel Martin, Isabel Roche, Jacob Madukakuzhy, Jim Dolan, Josita, Joe Mattam, Joe Pulickal, John Bosco, Joe Mekat, Leela Kottoor, Margaret Rodericks, Miriam K., Paul Raj, Ray Jacques, Rex Pai, Sebastian Inchody, Selma, Spiro Camilleri, Stella, Tom Palakudiyil, Vincent Bañón.

The constant complaint of the disciple to his Zen Master was, "you are hiding the final secret of Zen from me." And he refused to believe the Master's denials.

The Master one day took him for a walk along the hills. While they were walking they heard a bird sing.

"Did you hear that bird sing?" said the Master.

"Yes," said the disciple.

"Well, now, you know that I have hidden nothing from you."

"Yes," said the disciple.

—*The Song of the Bird,* p. 16

1

Tony was giving a prayer seminar, and I went to meet him during the interval. In the room I found him blowing soap bubbles into the air with a straw. "Look, look," he said, "how lovely, how fragile, how sparkling the bubbles are. And how they die without resistance. I want to die like that, fresh and lively." Tony's comment triggered in me a sense of life, its fleetingness and impermanence, and a desire to give my best: to delight in life and accept its transience. . . .

He wrote to me once:

> What is this mystery that we call life? We get attached to people, love them deeply and then we have to separate from them. . . . John 3: the theme of rebirth . . . one has to be born again . . . the Spirit comes from we know not where and goes we know not where. . . . We are born only to be separated. Because that is what birth is: a separation from our mothers' womb. And that is what rebirth is—a separation and a good-bye. We have to be constantly moving on from those who love us, constantly saying good-bye and being separated. Ultimately deep down in the roots of our being each one of us is alone. Finally we have to be separated by death, not only from our friends and loved ones, but even from our own body, from our own personality. . . . What part of us will remain? Perhaps that final part that no one can touch . . . mysterious and unknown . . . which we might call 'Spirit' . . . comes from we know not where and goes to we know not where. When we get in touch with that Spirit we are really reborn.

2

Tony would laugh at my worries and tell me, "Resign from the Mother Superiorship of the Universe." When I spoke to him about my resentment at the way some had treated me, he would say, "Human dignity needs to be respected: do not be a doormat to anyone. . . ." This simple truth helped me much.

One day when I went for a walk with him, he wanted to know what the group thought of him. After hearing my response he asked what I thought of him. Together with all the love and admiration I had for him, there were in him things I could not accept. I told him about them. He listened.

He spoke strongly about the way the Catholic Church controls its members. Hearing him I asked myself, "Am I taking a cue from the Church, and am I trying to control those I have to care for?" Today I am able to look at the Church with more realism, and examine my own ways.

Each time I was with Tony I was the only one who mattered to him. That was a great feeling. I could be just natural and free before him. I could speak with ease and share with him my most hidden thoughts. Nothing surprised him. . . .

He wanted me to be responsible for whatever I thought, felt, or did instead of putting the blame for my unhappiness on someone else.

The incidents narrated above, and many others, revealed to me a person who was often right and sometimes wrong, and who had a joy and empathy and wisdom and love. Experiencing these in him I have come to recognize and believe in the best in myself.

3

Early in a maxi-Sadhana session I was counseling James. At the end of it Tony made some comments. Then turning to me he asked:

TONY: What did you do for James?

BASIL: *He seems to have come to an awareness of some of his feelings.*

T: I asked you what you did for James.

B: *I helped him to understand his feelings.*

T: What are you doing with your hands? What are you feeling?

I had started tapping the floor with my hands unaware. I was nervous.

During a later session a woman in the group said she loved me and wanted to relate to me.

T: What are you feeling?

B: . . . *Happy.* . . .

T: What are you doing with your hands?

Unaware I had started tapping my right knee. I was nervous. I stopped it.

T: What are you doing with your left hand?

I had started tapping the left knee. I stopped that and tied my arms tightly across my chest.

T: What are you doing with your hands? Basil, don't push down joy. Don't tie yourself. Don't deny yourself love. Take in love. Give yourself permission to be joyful. Now, instead of pushing down your feelings wave your feelings up, wave your hands upward.

I waved. A freedom and a joy filled me, and I laughed in abandon.

Another occasion. Tony asked the group to describe the sensations each one was experiencing then. When I had finished Tony looked at me and said:

T: Are you aware you spoke only of touch sensations? Are you aware of the way you are sitting? Are you aware of the way your legs and hands are?

I was sitting crouched. I had my thighs tightly together and hands folded over them.

Thus began a process of becoming aware of feelings, of the body, of seeing the connection between feelings and actions, a process of owning up and integrating. For me this terrain is the same as that of the Ignatian "movement of spirits," of discernment and of decision making.

4

Midway through our Sadhana Tony said the following to me: "I have found you alive, vibrant and in fact very mature in many ways. However, I have been experiencing some discomfort and now I know why. My dear, emotionally you are a typical teenager seducing men right and left, top and bottom, and you are wondering why the men fall for you at every step." Well, that was definitely a mouthful, not easy to accept as I had considered myself half-a-saint already.

From the next session on Tony spared no effort to point out to me my seducing tactics—looks, pose, choice of words to communicate feelings, etc. . . .

MARRIAGE COUNSELOR TO FEMALE CLIENT: *Maybe your problem is that you have been waking up grumpy in the morning.*

CLIENT: *No, I always let him sleep.*

5

Jim is struggling, wanting to be independent, to live his own life, and at the same time not wanting to disappoint his many friends.

TONY: Get in touch with that pain of living it alone, of living with the truth, which will antagonize your friends.

JIM: *There will always be someone else who loves me.*

T: You are blaming, leaving a loophole: get in touch with the pain of really living it alone, not blaming them either for leaving you: stay with the pain.

J: *I wish I were not me now.*

T: Feel the pain of doing your own thing. If you blame you may feel better, but you are running away from that pain.

J: *Suddenly it occurred to me that in my province and in my work there I will be on my own.*

T: Again running away and soothing yourself with slogans. Imagine yourself sitting with the one you want to sit with and the others being angry at you for not choosing them.

J: *I feel like running away.*

T: When you are in your room go over the tape of this conversation and stay with the pain. It is real crucifixion . . . the grain of wheat will die, . . . and then true resurrection, and the true self will emerge. Let no drug divert you from or allow you to stop short of living: neither the drug of relationships, nor the drug of love—love is a sweetening of life, never a substitute for life—nor the drug of religion, nor of God, nor the drug of appreciation or praise or fulfilling the expectations of others. . . . Deepen your sense of rootedness, of being home. Feel the fear, the pain . . . then feel the strength. It is painful to go it alone. Sure. But there is no other way.

6

"Pain is neither positive nor negative: pain is of life. And life is growth and any growth has pain as one of its essential ingredients."

Such statements Tony used to repeat, especially in concrete situations of pain where he saw us struggling and spending much energy. In this way he led me to develop a tolerance of pain and the contradictions in life.

"If I immunize myself by all means against pain, then I will be shutting myself from intimacy and growth, from life itself."

Once I realized that I need not avoid pain at all cost, I began to breathe freely. I felt at ease to explore the pains of my life, like the separation of my parents. . . . I recognized the energy being released if only I learn to accept the inevitable and the factors over which I had no control. Initially with Tony pointing out this truth at crucial and vulnerable moments, and later becoming aware of it by myself, I was led into the frozen areas of my life. They began to have life and movement again.

"It's painful and I can take it, is a life-giving attitude."

"You can comply and have no pain, and be dead: You can be free and spontaneous and have pain, and be alive."

7

In North India there is the feast of *Raksha Bandhan.* A girl
ties a *rakhee*, an amulet of flowers or of ornamental paper or
silver string, on the wrist of her brother or a male friend. The
meaning is that the girl requests the man's brotherly care and
protection over her, and he agrees.

On Raksha Bandhan Day during the year of my Sadhana, a
woman in the group had a rakhee for each of the ten men in
the group. I brought two rakhees to the group. I tied one on
the wrist of Tony and the other on the wrist of a friend. Tony
burst out laughing and said, "It is easy to tie a rakhee on
everyone—none is left out; but it is difficult to choose one or
two from the group, is it not?"

8

"I will help you in your English," Tony said. It was December 1949. Both of us were Jesuit Junior students: he was nineteen; I was twenty-three and just come from Spain. "I want you to speak not only grammatically correct English, but even idiomatic English," he continued. Tony did correct my English for many years. He did it in such a way that he never made me feel inferior. It was an act of love.

I was appointed novice master, which I never would have dreamed of. When I met Tony he laughed his hearty laugh and said, "You will be an excellent novice master. Just be yourself." That helped me much to believe in myself.

I was given a big administrative assignment. Tony told me: "I think it is going to be too much for you. You will surely suffer much. However, how do you feel about it?" I said, "I see it as a challenge. I want to plunge into it." "Go ahead," said Tony, "but know that you are going to suffer along the way." I did suffer.

Tony once told me, "Because of the insistence in our Jesuit training that we must control our emotions, you are becoming a man of steel. There is so much warmth of feelings within you, but you repress it—never express it—you are not being your true self." I found this remark disturbing. "I know," I said, "but if I let go of my footing I may lose control of myself: once the dam is open I may be carried away in my own flood of feelings." Tony coolly said, "Your choice. Choose being a 'steel-man,' or a warm-hearted individual."

My Door Is Always Open is the title of a book we came across in our tertianship. "Wouldn't it be a beautiful motto for us priests about to begin our ministry," I said to Tony. He laughed and incisively said, "That is all right for Europe where no one ever goes to see a priest. But in India, if you leave your door open people will eat you up." They did.

A touchingly loving man. One who could gauge the strengths and limits of others, who could affirm and warn in detachment. One who left us free. Daring, not taking anything on authority. One who knew his power and the possible danger in that power.

Friend–Philosopher–Guide.

9

I had come for a weekend to Sadhana. At breakfast Tony asked me why I was so hung up about the Catholic establishment. I said I did not think it was healthy for anyone's spiritual growth to be plucked in adolescence to join a religious order, with vows of poverty, chastity, and obedience as binding, though there were exceptions like our saints. I nearly fell off my chair when Tony heartily agreed with my viewpoint. Then he challenged, "What alternative would you recommend?" I replied, "The ancient Indian asramas—the four stages where a person takes sanyas after being fulfilled as a householder." Again, he agreed with this, and added, "How do we incorporate that?" In these one-minute glimpses, I knew I was in front of a sage who had indeed transcended the traffic of religious competition and consumerism. He helped people to remove the psychological blocks in themselves . . . then the current of God's love would flow freely. At the same time he counseled, "Do not let your love of God interfere with love of your fellow-humans."

10

SEBASTIAN: *I have a great fear of God: when I imagine God I feel low, thrown down, small. I do tell people of God's mercy and goodness, but I don't feel at all that way.*

TONY: Who is frightening you?

S: *God is, he keeps me down looking so piercingly.*

T: Who is drawing that picture?

S: *I.*

T: Quite sure?

S: *Maybe I got it from someone, and I am putting it on God. Maybe he is that way.*

T: Maybe he is that way!

S: *Then I will be justified in my fear; yes, maybe he is that way or maybe I project that image onto him.*

T: Are you comfortable with that ambivalence or are you frightened?

S: *I am always in suspense about it.*

T: What and who and how God, Ultimate Reality, is, I do not know: I make an act of trust and occasionally I experience him as merciful. Yes, it could ultimately prove to be a cruel joke, but that doesn't rub me, it rubs you. You want to stop letting it rub you?

S: *I would like to, but I am afraid to let go, to take the step.*

T: Here a strength is needed which you now use against yourself. Whenever you start nagging yourself, being frightened, you put your strength on him to put yourself down. Job fought him, and in the end Job won. You are saying to yourself and you consider yourself worthless; and so many teachers, retreats, religious sermons, etc. . . . keep you convinced of that.

"Fear of God: it is our own cruelty and anger and strength that we project on God, on the other. Take that strength, even if it looks negative: it is your strength. Be aware of it, own it, act God, and you'll break through your paralyzing fear: you will be able to communicate with God, be able to listen to him and discover him."

11

I had done a lot of work on my problems of anger during the therapy sessions and by myself. There was still the feeling of nervousness and restlessness, of oppression.

TONY: What is oppressing you?

A: *It is something which prevents me from joy, from making decisions, which makes me doubt and procrastinate. Whenever it is not there I feel free and calm.*

T: Be the oppressive thing and talk. I will talk as the oppressed you.

A: *The picture of my father comes to me.*

T: Let it be your father or whatever: dramatize the oppressive side. Be the oppressor.

A: *I know what is good for you. You will lead your life as I tell you. I am the boss. I am in charge. Just you do what I want you to do. And don't grumble or I'll kick you.*

T: I won't obey.

A: *I'll kick you. You just dare.*

T: I'll defy you. I'll get by.

A: *Just try.*

T: I will defy you.

A: *Just try and we'll see.*

This continued for some time with Tony asking in between how I was feeling. My feeling gradually changed from nervousness to strength. Seeing this Tony said, "You broke through. You are frightened of the oppressor in you. The only way to be liberated is to accept that oppressor. When you have done that you are strong and you can afford to be gentle and understanding. If not, you will come out too strongly, too harshly and people will resent you. The exercises you did earlier have helped you to get in touch with your anger and the strength it holds. Now you need to continue identifying with the strength of the oppressor in you, and you will come out in your activities harmonious."

"The person who is open to the bully in himself is not likely to act as a bully: one who is not familiar with it, will act the bully. It is important to be in touch with and to accept the ugly side in oneself."

"You will no longer be frightened of God the day you can become the God you are frightened of."

12

During a renewal session I told Tony directly, without hesitation and fear: "I cannot stick the behavior of my Superior. He is full of partiality and prejudice. This bugs me to no end."

Tony said: "You can work on this problem in three steps: (1) Who has the problem? He or you? (2) Are you ready to give this man permission to behave as he behaves? (3) Where's the problem?"

I realized I had the problem. I admitted that. This brought me to the second step. Tony asked me to leave the group, go by myself and begin to give permission to my Superior to be himself, being in touch with what I was feeling in the process. I did this for half an hour, then went to rejoin the group. Tony asked for feedback. I told him I felt lighter, freer, stronger. The expectations had vanished. Giving freedom to others I experienced freedom and power in me.

"So many of our actions in communities and in formation come from intolerance: So much of our preaching and morality is a veiled form of intolerance."

It is very warm and reassuring to know that when you get married, no matter what comes along, you will always have somebody at your side to blame it on.

13

I was not getting out of life what I knew it was offering me. On the contrary I felt life increasingly to be a burden, a drag. I was handling some of my problems poorly.

When I told Tony about this—it was actually my first meeting with him—he asked me to imagine I was sitting with Christ and Christ was asking me to describe my finest qualities. I did. I thought I was quite generous in praise of my talents. Then Tony asked me to tell Jesus my faults, etc. . . .

At the end of the exercise Tony said that I was much more eloquent in reciting my faults than I was in outlining my good qualities.

Simple as this interaction was, it somehow brought about in me a major shift. That was the beginning for me of waking up, of awareness.

14

I was in my early fifties, and I had been a respected priest in the Society of Jesus for many years. In my first therapy from Tony during my maxi-Sadhana, I spoke about a difficulty I had with a person. Tony helped me and slowly moved me to own up to my anger. I was surprised to learn that I was angry and had been fostering the anger without awareness and that I had not forgiven the person for a long time. This helped much. Lack of forgiveness continues to pester me. Now I am aware, and I forgive more easily.

One day Tony called me. Very honestly he told me he was feeling threatened and jealous because I seemed to be walking on air ever since a good friend of mine had arrived a few days earlier. I laughed aloud. "Shanti, I am serious," he said, "I am feeling jealous and I am suffering and I am a neurotic."

"One's strength is not in being adult, but in being honest. There is great strength in honesty, seeing and admitting what one experiences and what one wants now, whatever it may be."

15

In one session I spoke about my problem of being timid. Tony advised me, "During the next week take the initiative in starting conversations or joining conversations which are going on." I tried. Often people ignored me, and I felt very self-conscious and pained. When I reported this at the end of the week to Tony, he asked, "What do you do to get what you want?"

In challenging situations I tend to be very weak. A friend gave negative feedback to me in the group. I sat there smiling. This angered him and the whole group. I, on the other hand, felt let down by them and alone. I could not understand why they reacted this way. At the close of the session Tony said to me, "You go through the embarrassment and the pain and the self-pity. Become aware of the self-talk and the conditioning which is producing them. Do not go back to your room and cry. You need to find other ways of responding."

Over a number of sessions I had made several attempts to get out of a deep-seated fear of my mother. At one session Tony asked me to shout "no" to my mother. My voice was barely audible. The more my companions urged me to shout louder, the more feeble my voice grew. Finally Tony said, "Your mother is very strong in you, is she not?"

Different responses at different times. I continue to refer to them in my efforts to be freer.

16

It had often seemed to me people were taking advantage of me, making unreasonable demands, not understanding my needs, constraints, etc. . . . . This was acute in the case of my friendships. I wanted them and at the same time I felt they were impinging on my freedom. I couldn't say no to my friends lest I displease them.

After hearing something similar from me on several occasions, Tony said, "Do you really want to hear the truth? You don't want to change. What you really want is an assurance from me that you are right and every one else is wrong, and it is because of others that you are suffering, miserable, etc."

A few days later, a week before Christmas, Tony held out a plastic plate to me and said, "This is my Christmas present for you," and he laughed. The plate had a picture of a little girl seated on the pot. "Do you recognize the little girl? It is you. You neither ——— nor get off the pot."

The message now was very clear. It was indeed difficult to accept that the problems were my own making, and if I wanted to be happy I needed to change.

"Stop acting like a fool!"

"I am not acting."

"What awareness! . . ."

17

I remember one of the sayings of Tony about Jesus and Gandhiji: "Jesus preached what he lived: Gandhiji lived what he preached. The first was very much alive because his teaching came from the experience of life. The second was logical and reasoned and consequently his life had much less flavor—what was first reasoned out, was then worked out in life."

Without denigrating the latter, Tony put a premium on the former. "Life and love are there for those who dare to take risks and not for the mere spectator."

For me a striking example of this process is the following. During my mini-Sadhana in the late seventies, Tony talked on man-woman friendship among the religious. "Don't just talk about it, experience it and learn. . . . I know such friendships often lead to physical contacts. See that as part of the growth process. However, friendship among religious does not require physical expressions. These can be often harmful, especially when used as substitute for honest personal communication."

I had my own reactions to all this which I kept to myself. When some years later during a mini-Sadhana I clearly affirmed that relationship with women was not for me, Tony challenged me: "You are talking from principles, from your mind: you are not in touch with your feelings, your heart." I was impressed by Tony's arguments and his respect for my growth, yet I preferred to live on the mind level and would not take the plunge into experience.

Years later during an annual retreat I suddenly found myself faced with a terrible choice: I could either become a cynical, intellectual, unalive Jesuit, or relate with women as Tony had mentioned about ten years earlier. I took the second.

It has not been an easy road. I had to find my own way. Tony's stress on awareness, on being present to the here and now, on honestly listening to one's inner voice and taking personal responsibility has helped me much in this.

Love is said to be blind, but I know lots of fellows who can see twice as much in their sweethearts as I can. . . .

18

I once met Tony to talk about my relationship with one of the men in the group. It was the early stage of friendship and I was going through an inner struggle, not sure whether or not to proceed with it, change its movement, or drop it altogether. After I had spoken of how and when it started and how it was going, Tony raised a few questions. Having heard my responses he said, "Go ahead, go full steam ahead." I did.

It is now seventeen years that this friendship has continued. Thanks to the insight and support I received at that time I can call this relationship one of the greatest graces of my life.

In this matter as well as in others, a parable which Tony gave in one of the sessions and the questions he put have been providing valuable guidance to me.

> In a particular desert land peaches were very scarce. Some holy people of the land had a revelation which they put down in the following code: "Thou shalt not eat more than two peaches a day." Later some found the means to convert the desert into a garden. Trees started flourishing, peaches grew in plenty, so much so that they were falling from the trees and rotting on the ground. The young people began to rebel against the law on peaches, but the holy people were determined to maintain the law as they claimed it had been revealed by God. There were some people who ate more than two peaches a day and they were feeling guilty. Others also ate more than two peaches and they didn't feel guilty. Those among the young people who proclaimed "It is all right to eat more than two peaches a day" were punished.

The questions Tony put for the group's reflection were the following: Does your own code of morality stand up to reason? Does it work in practice or does it bring more inner tension than peace? Does it make you a less loving, a less happy person? Where does it go against common sense, and if it does, how do you deal with that?

19

I came to Sadhana after many years of work among people and in the training of religious. I was successful. I had read and liked the writings of John of the Cross and Teresa of Avila. I had a Christ-centered and Trinitarian spirituality, I believed.

In one Sadhana session, friendship among the religious was the topic of discussion. I said in my usual confident manner: "I don't need any. I have Christ, and that is enough."

Tony looked at me and said, "I don't like your Christ. He has dehumanized you." I was shaken. The centerpiece of my spirituality, Christ, was being attacked. And I, who have given myself so tirelessly to the poor . . . dehumanized?

Later one day I complained to Tony: "You are pulling down every one of my beliefs. You are leaving me with no support." He said, "I do this with very few people."

In the months which followed we learned to probe into the truth of our beliefs, assumptions, self-understandings. I saw, for example, when I said "I don't care what people think of me," I did in fact deeply care.

Beginning then I have lost many of my dearly held beliefs. And I have lost much of the aggressiveness, defensiveness, and insecurity I used to have. And I experience a great sense of freedom and oneness with all humans, with all creation. Christ and the Trinity are in my life now; so are deeply joyful friendships, and fun and play.

20

In one session John said, "I have a friend whom I love deeply. To my surprise I also experience resentment toward him now and then. I go out of my way to show my love to him, but he seems to take me often for granted and I have a nagging feeling that I am giving too much. I do not like myself for that."

"There is too much goodwill in you," Tony remarked, "too much spirituality, and you get tied down. In friendship one must be able to say the following: I accept you, I'll support you, you can count on me. And I want you to reciprocate my love. I want you to be honest with me."

"Friendship is like a dance. If you are stationary, I cannot dance. In that case I will leave you. My freedom I will not sacrifice. It may cause me pain, but that does not matter."

"You have to be ready to risk the relationship in order to keep it."

21

Toward the end of our maxi-Sadhana in March 1977, Tony gave this very wise counsel: "In retreats keep off fostering relationships. To be trying to develop relationships during a retreat is simply against professional ethics. Avoid all touch— it is against professional ethics. In the highly artificial situation of a retreat the usual retreatant is very dependent on you: you can manipulate the person to do whatever you want, even to fall in love with you. In a situation where there is a possibility of continuing the relationship and you are attracted to that person and really want a relationship, it might develop imperceptibly. But actively developing the relationship is not for the time of the retreat."

22

One day about three months into our Sadhana course, Tony seriously announced to the group: "I have decided that from today I will be one of the group just like anyone else. Except during therapy or similar situations when I want to proceed without interference, we are equals with regard to the right to relate to members of the group, to contribute to or interrupt the sessions."

I said, "Bullshit, Tony, that's bullshit. How can you say we are on equal ground when you well know you stand head and shoulders above us. Your announcement is a cruel joke."

There was a moment of silence. Then Tony lashed out at me: "That's the trouble with you, you cannot believe, don't dare to believe in your own strength and potential, behaving like chickens." I had never seen Tony that indignant.

It has taken me a long time to come to see why he reacted that way. He was right.

I needed approval from Tony. He was my god. During a session in 1976 some members in the group were asking Tony for his feedback. This sounded nice, and I waited my turn, with anxiety. "What do you think of me, Tony?" I asked. "Nothing to say," Tony replied, "you don't need my approval." That was a bomb that hit me hard. A mixture of feelings arose. It was left to me to recognize the message.

During one Sadhana renewal in Lonavla, my "number one" friend from Sadhana days was present and also another friend. The former who was feeling uneasy pressed me to declare which one of the two was the number one! I declined to play the "number game." This kept her dissatisfied. Tony called the two of us to his room.

After openly telling each other our feelings and expectations she still felt unhappy. Tony turned toward her and caringly yet firmly said to her: "Do you realize you are second to none? What is important is that you realize that in worth you are second to none."

EVE: *Adam, do you love me?*

ADAM: *Who else?*

23

It happened in a session of maxi-Sadhana. One day, reluctantly, I presented a personal problem to the group. Everyone bombarded me. As a finale Tony exploded a dynamite, shattering all my defenses. After the ordeal I couldn't eat or drink, and I threw up repeatedly. I felt exhausted and lonely.

Tony had given strict orders to the group not to meet me at all. However a "good Samaritan" came to console me. Tony chased him away. The following day Tony said in the group that he loved me and knew that I had the resources to face the agony of growth. The painful silence was an experience of realizing my own irrational views and of gaining growth-promoting wisdom.

With cruel compassion Tony had in a masterly fashion administered therapy to heal me. It was a turning point in my life.

I was taking therapy from Tony in the group. Gradually I sank into a depression of sorts. One day, two days, several days—I continued in the depression. And I began to feel very angry with Tony. Why doesn't he help me out? More indirectly than directly I communicated this anger to him. All he said was, "I love you much. It pains me to see you like this. You have a lot of strength within you." I had learned something very valuable.

24

I was a person who had many cherished "shoulds and musts," to the point of being legalistic. Through several of Tony's programs which I attended over the years and his personal guidance, many of these "shoulds" have fallen by the wayside. He challenged me to look into the many absolutes I had made for myself.

At first I resisted his challenge. It threatened my security, and I argued with him. He was patient and understanding, yet he continued to encourage me to explore my fears in reexamining my position. Eventually I did reexamine some of them.

The consequence of this was quite frightening in the beginning. Many accustomed signposts in my inner road disappeared. For a time I was at a loss as to where I was going. Yet, slowly a new and deeper self emerged. I became more inner-directed, centered within. I began to take more responsibility for my life and actions. Many rules and regulations got relativized in the process. Some of these I still observe—more as "club rules" rather than as absolutes.

Today I feel much freer within, much more deeply committed to my God and to my call.

25

During one session of my maxi-Sadhana, Tony and I had the following dialogue:

A: *I feel threatened by the prospect of being free and of leaving others free. And I resent you for imposing your views, brainwashing and throwing us into doubt.*

TONY: The more free and secure I became, the less proselytising I did. Nobody can make you doubt or impose something on you. Indicate one area in which you want to be free.

A: *God. I want to be free of this God-Father.*

T: Tell me what that means.

A: *I believe God loves me and cares for me. At the same time there is an uneasiness in me about him. I resent him.*

T: Suppose God-Father is a myth, a concept to explain a reality that is ineffable. Now go beyond the myth and go to the ineffable. In fantasy go as it were on a spacial journey, into the reality beyond the myth. What happens?

A: *. . . I feel myself go . . . the others are far . . . I feel strong and cold and a sense of missing. . . .*

T: Stay with the sense of coldness, of missing, and that sense of strength.

A: *. . . I am a robot with a warm flame inside which wants to spread.*

T: Be the robot with the flame and stand in front of your dad. What happens? (We had earlier worked on my unfinished relationship with my dad.)

A: . . . *As I stand here I am irritated . . . angry with my dad . . . resentful. . . . I want to push him out of the way with my iron arm . . . and then the flame in me dies. . . .*

T: You were not in touch with the strength in you when you were in front of your dad. Be again in front of him, and be in touch with the flame in you, with your strength.

A: . . . *The flame wants to grow. . . . I am frightened . . . there is struggle in me . . . will he extinguish it? . . . I go blank. . . .*

T: Do this again. Stand alone before your dad and recapture the flame. Spend time on this.

Slowly I discovered how my resentment of God-Father, of my dad, of Tony were all of a piece: it found its nourishment in a whole set of experiences and inherited images of God, and of self, of beliefs and principles regarding moral and social relationships. Becoming aware of these and freeing myself of them in small painful steps, I trust I am on my way to the ineffable of which Tony spoke.

26

During the retreat in my days of Sadhana I became aware of something stifling me: the congregation to which I belonged was binding my freedom. Though shocked at myself and upset at this turn of events, I strongly felt like leaving my congregation.

"Let it lie low, do not worry about it now," Tony said to me. I found it difficult to do so. I had wanted to thrash it out there and then, yet I heeded Tony's advice.

And then one day ten months later, I woke up one morning with the inner knowledge of being in the right place: the stifling feeling had disappeared.

Why had I wanted to leave the congregation? Why did I suddenly feel at home now? Gradually it dawned on me that my problem was not with the congregation but with my mother. Over the past ten months I had spent a great deal of time working out that problem. Tony sensed this, and that is why he asked me to lie low and not to worry about that urge to leave the congregation.

27

Once I was very much troubled by a dream which was very vivid. I entered into a big church, where lots of people were participating in the Mass. After a few minutes I wanted to get away. Going through a side door I found myself in another big church. Some people were there praying. I felt an anxiety in me because I was in another church. I hurried out and found myself in yet another church. It was silent, there was nobody in this church. I was very much upset. I rushed out through a side door only to find myself in a fourth church which was cold, ancient, and dilapidated. There was green moss on the walls. There was no Blessed Sacrament. All the statues had been removed from the altar and put into a side room. I was very much frightened. I was caught in the church. As I was looking for some way to get out, the statue of Saint Paul from the side room started moving. It came out mumbling things like a madman. I was terribly frightened. I got up breathing heavily and perspiring. Whenever I remembered the dream and told someone, my whole body reacted.

Some time later I had a chance to meet Tony, and I gave him an account of my dream. "How many years have you been novice master?" he asked. I said, "Three." "And the next year is the fourth," he said. "The four churches signify the four years of your novice mastership. You have been caught in this. You have been becoming lonelier day by day. People disappeared as you entered the second and the third one. The fourth church is a warning given to you. If you do not care, you may have a breakdown . . . a mumbling Saint Paul."

As he spoke to me everything fell into its place. I was doing a good job as a novice master, but at a heavy cost. I was the first novice master of the new novitiate. All the eyes of the province were on me and on the novitiate. My friends advised me to be very circumspect and prudent to make our novitiate a success. I framed my own rules so as to be a good novice master.

By nature I like to move around and meet people. I curtailed all my movements and stayed in the novitiate most of the time. I stopped going out for films. I was losing interest in meeting my women friends. Though my inner self told me that I was not a novice and I need not follow all the practices meant for novices, I followed them to give a good example to them. All these were strains upon me. My prayer was getting dry.

Tony suggested to me that either I quit my novice mastership or change my ways drastically. I could not quit my job. I changed quite a few of my ways. I took opportunities to move out, I renewed my contacts with friends, I started going out for films once in a while. I relaxed some of the self-imposed rules. New life rushed into me. I believe I was also a better novice master.

Tony's openness and courage to question even the basic things, his insights into reality and the Eastern flavor of his spirituality seasoned my spiritual attitudes and enlightened me on various issues.

28

Freeing myself of religion, of God, of an oppressive morality has been an important aspect of my growth during these last twenty years. It has been strongly accelerated during my Sadhana days in the mid-seventies as Tony would focus on these aspects in various ways.

During that time and to the end of his life Tony was fond of quoting approvingly some author who said in effect: In my long life I have had many sufferings, but religion is not one of them.

"Do I really need a religious 'upsetting myself' in order to see the wrong in a situation and do something about it?" Tony would say. "The purpose of so many of our exhortations, preachings, moral injunctions, etc. . . . . is to upset ourselves into action, to badger ourselves into doing good. Often I help my neighbor because Jesus asks me to do so, for his sake, because he did likewise, because of a text from Scripture, because it would be a sin not to help, etc. But do I need this drug to be a compassionate person, to be human? Letting the reality around me, what I see and hear, motivate me is so much healthier."

Underneath my own guilt and anger and restlessness often I have found to exist a religious cause. Tony helped me to look courageously into this and free myself.

"So much of our negative emotions and problems like dissatisfaction, guilt, restlessness, feeling inadequate, . . . come because the moralistic side of us continuously goads us to change and to perform. This inner violence breeds violence outside. So much of the dying to oneself, vital in spiritual growth, is wrongly identified with the killing of oneself. Religion that aims at making us good, ends up making us evil. Whereas the religion known as freedom makes us good because it does not create this inner conflict."

"The reason I climb mountains is because they are there!"

"That is the reason everybody else goes around them!"

29

I made my tertianship Long Retreat with Tony. His daily conferences were full of insights and challenges. Toward the end of the second week he gave a conference on the Prayer of Faith or Silence which touched me. When I shared this with him, he just said, "Stop meditating." Not quite understanding what he meant, I resorted to simpler affective prayer. At my next personal meeting with him he told me: "Cut it all out—no thinking, no imagining, no expressing, etc." This left me for a couple of days in sheer frustration and helplessness till there was an unexpected breakthrough—a powerful and prolonged experience of prayer in-depth without any effort of mine.

Even after twenty years I am deeply grateful to Tony. He listened to me, understood me, intervened at the right time. The effect of this grace has been far-reaching—beyond my retreat—and progressively touching every part of my being and life.

30

One day during one of the Sadhana therapy sessions, Sushila was talking about her problem of deep depression. After some interaction with her, Tony talked to the group about different ways to get out of a depression. Then he was silent, looking at Sushila. Suddenly he said, "Has God too walked out of your life?" She started weeping. Then she narrated how God who had been so near had disappeared from her life, and everything now seemed so empty. The group was silent, moved.

When it was over, Tony spoke to us about spiritual depression, different from other psychological depressions. One of the group members asked Tony how he had come to the conclusion that this was spiritual depression. "Deep inside I felt it," he responded.

One day Tony said, "A teacher teaches, but a guru guides a person to discover self, God, and reality. We need gurus, who have experienced God, persons of experience who can guide others to mysticism. It is all right to learn counseling, theology, spirituality, etc., but don't stop there: become mystics, gurus." Tony believed and took pains to make us see that mysticism is for us too. He helped us to recognize these mystical experiences in ourselves and in others.

31

Once during a therapy session a priest was telling Tony that he was feeling sad but could not put his finger on the reason for it. He said that he had been feeling that way now and then for the last three or four years. Tony told him, "Tell me whatever comes to your mind about the last five years of your life." The priest went on for about twenty minutes. I could not get any clue about the source of his sadness. Nor did the others seem to get any. When the priest had finished Tony asked him to repeat a particular sentence he had said some ten minutes earlier. The priest repeated, "I was given the transfer order and asked to report to the new job in three days. I reported in two." Tony then asked him, "Aren't you sad that you could not take time to say good-bye to the parishioners you loved so much?" The priest began to cry. The rest of the therapy was routine.

32

Once I asked Tony, "What is contemplation?" He didn't say a word. Some days later the two of us had supper near the lake: full moon, its light playing on the gentle waves of the lake. We sat in absolute silence as if nothing else existed. We almost forgot to eat the supper we had brought along. As we got up to go back Tony turned to me and said, "What is contemplation?"

One afternoon sitting under the trees outside the old Sadhana building we were discussing different topics. Suddenly Whitey, our dog, who had been sleeping nearby was on its feet, all alert, barking at a monkey up the tree. The dog was absolutely involved, and its eyes were fixed even on the slightest movement of the monkey. No other world existed for him, except the movement of that monkey. Tony asked me, "Did you see Whitey? . . . "

Tony and I went for a walk and we sat under a tree on a small hill. We chatted about many things—rather I was chattering away from the head, rather than from the heart. Tony had made me aware of this way of mine on a number of occasions. I often would forget.

Finally we came to the topic of awareness. Suddenly he said: "Stop talking. Listen, see, experience the beauty of the place, the trees, the sounds . . . the surroundings. They have a lot to tell you." The conversation stopped. I became peaceful, silent.

33

The book *Sadhana—A Way to God* had just been released. With a twinkle in his eyes Tony shared with me how he visualized people buying the book, wanting to know what the Sadhana course was all about, and being disappointed. "Do they think we are doing prayer exercises all the time?" he quipped.

No, Sadhana as I experienced it is not doing prayer exercises all the time: it is a way of looking at reality "prayerfully." As one of my companions put it, "Sadhana deals with God, spiritual problems, growth, and people in the context of daily life."

34

One session during my mini-Sadhana was a turn in my life. I had brought to Tony and the group a problem: I felt I always loved people more than they loved me. . . . I cannot forget Tony's response: "Did you ever tell any one how much you love him, her?" My answer was no. "Then how do they know how much you love them? and how do you know if they are not just doing the same to you? . . . so no real communication," Tony replied. Simple as the dialogue was, it made an impact in my life.

I have a deep love for prayer—I pray much in my retreats and always in full desert style—and yet I had come to drop most of my formal prayers. This contradiction in my life bothered me, and I brought it up in an open encounter with the whole group. In response to this Tony made me close my eyes and be in touch with what went on in me, while he repeated the statement "I was wrong and I am deceiving myself." I felt terribly bad at first, then better, and then totally calm and told him I deeply felt he did not understand me, and I did not feel I was wrong. Then he repeated the statement "All of us are telling you that you are wrong and deceiving yourself, and all specialists in spirituality are telling you the same." Tony asked me how I had felt. I told him, "Terrible at first, then more and more calm, and then totally calm: a feeling within me that they did not grasp what my prayer really was." Tony added nothing more. Yet this interaction caused in me a deepening of my life and prayer.

35

D: *I am not praying. At the same time I experience a desire to pray. In fact whenever I prayed I have felt good. And yet I pray rarely. "One ought to pray," "A religious should pray. . . ."—are such rules bugging me? I don't think so. I believe "oughts" and "shoulds" don't govern me.*

TONY: Do you want to pray today?

D: *Yes.*

T: When? . . . at what time? . . . in which place? . . . in what posture? . . .

When the definite possibility of praying stared me into the eyes I started losing my nerve.

Then Tony said, "You have a genuine desire to pray. But you don't sit quiet long enough to let that desire surface in its full strength: you would distract yourself. Sit for five minutes every day and get in touch with your desire to pray, as you did a while ago. Asking yourself 'What is happening? What's it I gain? What's it I want? etc. . . .' can help the process. Let the desire for prayer emerge in its strength and clarity and reasonableness; then distractions, other attractions will fall in place. You will pray, gladly paying the price. Give the muddy pool a chance to settle down. You will see clear water. You will love it. . . . You will pray."

36

Experience is central to Ignatian spirituality. In his own search and discourse Tony tried to bring experience back to the center stage of any spiritual quest, of any growth.

As I look back at the long association I had with Tony from our days together in studies, through Sadhana, prayer seminars, and personal contacts, some things clearly stand out in my mind: his challenge to live the now moment, the centrality of personal experience, and the relentless pursuit after truth. Truth here is not propositional truth but my truth as life itself makes known to me. This pursuit of truth and experience then become transformative forces in life.

This aspect of Tony's teaching challenged me immensely, and it still does.

37

I had done my theology during the years soon after Vatican II. The learning on Faith and Revelation had been quite a challenge for me as it helped me to go beyond the mere stating and understanding of conceptual truths. Yet, a few years later during my Sadhana course in the mid-seventies, I received an even greater challenge through Tony's insight that belief is different from faith. Faith is intimately connected with our lived experience.

One cannot easily put one's life experience in words or concepts; similarly, faith defies expression. Faith cannot be captured by beliefs.

This insight seeped into me powerfully. It made me respect experience "faithfully," explore it with reverence, and discover the depth it held out to me. My reading of Scripture became much more alive and real. I could now confidently challenge my own belief system. More and more I live by faith.

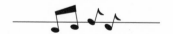

"When belief is taken for faith, one loses faith."

38

After dealing with me in therapy for some time, Tony detected my tendency to "correct" situations and people. Looking me in the eye, he said: "John, you will attain real peace and 'salvation' the day you accept the world and everyone and everything in it as being as perfect as it could possibly be now. There is nothing to correct, nothing to make better. When you become really aware of this, you will have inner peace."

On different occasions and in different ways Tony came back to this same theme of Salvation Now.

39

One day, the day before the end of our Sadhana, a sister in our group wanted to work on a personal difficulty. Tony patiently listened, and then he drew her attention to some incongruency in her behavior. When she defended herself he directly told her she had been escaping real personal work during the whole course. He was explicit, firm, and very much uninvolved. In the end he left it to her to go on or not. We were hoping she would take the plunge. After a nervous few moments, she smiled and said: "I'll take it up later." Tony accepted her decision and went on with someone else.

"Silence in counseling can be a powerful weapon to break down hidden resistance. I interpret it as the greatest tribute to the human person. To wait in respectful silence for the moment of readiness. By no means a waste of time."

40

As a provincial I used to send quite a number of sisters for help to Tony. Some profited, others seemed to have profited at first, but then relapsed. This caused frustration in me. I also used to be questioned about the wisdom of sending people for help and to Sadhana. One day I mentioned this to Tony: "Is it possible for people to change? Do basic dispositions change?"

He said, "I think, as I grow older, I become so resigned to the fact that people are the way they are, and one might as well accept the fact and learn to live with it. I think most of our troubles with people come from our demanding or expecting or hoping that they will change: they do not."

PSYCHIATRIST: *I have treated you for six months and now you are cured. You will no longer have delusions of grandeur and imagine that you are Napoleon.*

PATIENT: *That's wonderful. I can hardly wait to go home and tell Josephine the good news.*

41

I had completed writing a book, and I asked Tony to write an introduction for it. He agreed at once, told me to leave the typescript with him as he would send the introduction directly to my publisher. The publisher never received it. Instead, I received a letter from Tony in which he said, "I have changed my mind. Your book deserves a better introduction than I can write at the moment. And you don't need it: the book will sell well anyhow." I knew I should feel slighted, disappointed, and angry, but I could not succeed in feeling bad about the letdown. Tony had done something more important for me than writing an introduction; he had taught me that he was supremely free, even from his own pledged word. I smiled to myself and treasured the lesson.

42

My first encounter with Tony was in September 1974. After a decade of priestly life I was feeling disillusioned about priesthood and its functioning in the Society of Jesus. I had almost made up my mind to leave the Society. As a last effort "to save my vocation" the then General Arrupe suggested to me that I make a Long Retreat under Tony's direction. I agreed. I was greatly impressed by the person of Tony, particularly by his love of poverty and the simplicity of his life. He challenged me in such a way that I stayed on in the Society.

My second encounter was during a one-month course in Pune. During the course I realized in particular that I had too many illusions about myself, too many prejudices about others, and many false images of God. This gave me a freedom and fearlessness, the kind of which I had never experienced before.

April–May 1979 was a memorable period in my life. But for Tony's persistent encouragement I may not have gone through a risky open-heart surgery. As I was recuperating in the hospital Tony happened to be nearby giving a prayer seminar. He found time to visit me and spend two nights with me in the hospital. I was very much taken up by this fine gesture of companionship.

And then in 1985 I went to do a long Sadhana. What struck me was the great changes that had come about in Tony. He had become one very much involved with everything that was real, who enjoyed a good joke and relished a good meal, who laughed boisterously and enjoyed every minute thoroughly, spent time with people and with nature. I felt Tony had become one with another world. Could we call it the world of the spirits?

My last meeting with Tony was on May 27, 1987, after he had just finished the prayer seminar at Pune. I could see the fatigue in his eyes and a certain amount of weariness in his whole demeanor. Yet, all through the seminar itself Tony was in his element, enjoying every minute.

And then on June 1, I heard that he had died in New York. On the morning of June 13, I saw his mortal remains. The rich and varied memories of the past thirteen years flashed across my mind. The mystery of an eventful life swallowed up by the other mystery of death. . . . He could have lived another twenty years. . . . "Good news, bad news, who knows. . . ."

43

During our mini-Sadhana renewal in 1984, in a discussion on the person of Christ, Tony said, "For me Christ is someone who has been true to his inner promptings, who restlessly followed his inner voice. Our call to be Christs here and now is to be answered by our relentless search to follow our own inner voice, as Christ did."

These words opened for me a new dimension of following Christ. This means that I am to follow my own experience and the light that comes from my informed reflection on the experience. Authority is not sacrosanct.

The responsibility for my growth is on my shoulders.

44

We were talking in the group on the multi-religious Indian situation, the salvation of those who had lived on earth before Christ came, of those who lived after he came but who never heard of him, and the Church's insistence that salvation comes through Christ alone. Would this position meet the same fate as an earlier one that only those could be saved who were subject to the jurisdiction of the pope? We were raising these and similar questions. Tony had kept quiet. Then he gave his own answer.

The statement about the uniqueness of Christ and other similar statements are mythological or poetic. They cannot be taken in a purely rationalistic and literal way. A reflection which I read recently can aptly be used here. When a man says about his wife that she is the most beautiful woman in the world, he is not making this statement in comparison to any other woman. He is making a statement that is highly personal. As long as it remains at that level it is very meaningful. When he goes and calls his neighbor and tells him, "My wife is more beautiful than your wife," then the statement begins to be offensive.

One can say with all sincerity that Christ is unique for me, that he is the most meaningful person and reality for me. This is poetic and romantic and very true. I have no need to worry about the comparative place of Christ in relation to other religious personalities. I am only relating an experience that I have.

I was brought to the core of religious reality, namely, the centrality of personal experience in any sharing of religious truths.

45

"If I had to introduce Jesus, I would say the following," Tony said one day, "He forgets the things done against him. He finds something positive also in those who are against him. He has a very good memory of the good things done to him. He gives his fragrance to those who wound him as the tree gives its fragrance to those who cut it. 'Be compassionate as your heavenly Father is compassionate' expresses well who he is."

THE BISHOP TOURIST AT THE SEA OF GALILEE: *How much is it to cross the lake?*

THE BOATSMAN: *Fifty dollars.*

BISHOP: *Fifty dollars! No wonder Jesus decided to walk it.*

46

Tony would make comments like the following: "So and so said that you are charming. . . ." or "When you first spoke I thought this is a real woman, but look what you have done to yourself now." The latter statement was made when I was not coming out positively about someone or something. It made me realize the gift I had of being positive but which I had allowed to be lost. The former statement, though seemingly trivial, was not trivial for me at the moment when I was establishing my inner strength based on my lovability, etc. . . . gifts which the Lord had given me but I had made little of.

In Sadhana days I was engrossed with my own psychological growth which had been ignored earlier. As I grow in age I seek to integrate with my faith experience all the growth I have made in life. For me this growth now is a reaching to the point of being like Christ.

This is the challenge I have gotten from Tony: to grow is to outgrow my fears and anxieties coming from an unexamined conditioning, to understand the impact this conditioning has on my present life, to realize how this conditioning keeps me an adolescent even in my mid-life.

47

1986–87: The last maxi-Sadhana with Tony. One incident I like to single out, as it keeps vibrating and finding its way in my life.

In one of the sessions Tony asked me, "Are you aware how cruel you are?" I was taken aback and could not accept myself being a cruel person. Someone who knew me as a gentle person tried to defend me, but Tony was firm in his remark. I took a while to understand what he meant by such a statement. It was regarding my difficulty in saying "no" to others— I wanted to please others and make peace with everyone around. With Tony's guidance I was able to have some understanding of this gentle, cruel me.

A few months ago, 1992 that is, I was in a session and my counselor asked me a similar question: "Are you aware of the two selves you entertain in your life—your best self and your disowned self?" I had been spending so much of my energy looking for approval, trying to do the right thing at the right time. My thoughts flew at once to the room in Sadhana, and I relived the entire session with Tony. I realized how much energy I was still spending looking for approval, trying to do the right thing at the right time. Noticing what was happening the counselor invited me to talk about it, which I gladly did.

48

We had talked about the need for change in the Church, the Society, etc. On August 21, 1980, Tony wrote, "My assessment of the situation is really the same as yours: we will not, after all our efforts, be able to achieve much . . . but I think I take something of the Hindu attitude that that is precisely the way things are meant to be . . . here has always to be an eternal struggle between the good and the bad . . . and both forces have to be more or less equally balanced . . . there has to be more or less the same proportion of cockle and wheat in the field of the kingdom . . . and so I don't feel too pessimistic. I am satisfied to do my thing, to dance my dance . . . and have done with it. According to a nice sentence I read somewhere, 'A bird does not sing because it has an answer. It sings because it has a song.' So I am content to sing my song, even though often the whole thing seems meaningless. . . ."

49

I was once telling Tony during my therapy session in Sadhana how I worry about what people think about me. He asked me if I had heard the story of the elephant coming to town. The elephant goes right along without so much as bothering to observe what people are thinking and doing. Whereas the little dog barks at every other dog it meets and at people who come in the opposite direction. I still have a drawing of the elephant which one Sadhanite made for me that very day.

"Think of happiness as a state of inner liberty. Forget the word *happiness* altogether. Substitute it with *inner liberty*. Inner liberty is true happiness."

50

"And all shall be well." In *Sadhana—A Way to God,* Tony describes this as the loveliest and most consoling sentence that he has ever read. It is the same sentence that we find on his tomb, capturing his life's message: the deep conviction that all shall be well, that life's inner force can be trusted because the God of life is a God of love, of unconditional love.

The earliest incident when the truth of this conviction was brought home to me was in 1976. It was the time when as a young seminarian I had begun my studies. I was anxious about what I would be doing as a Jesuit. I recall Tony sharing with me the changes that had come along in his life: how the journey had taken turns and directions not envisaged earlier. For me the point of the sharing was: what is important is not having every step of the journey clearly marked out, but entering into the journey with the readiness to live life to the fullest at that particular phase of the journey. The rest can be left to life and to God, because under his loving gaze all shall be well.

There have been several other occasions in my life when I had to be reminded about this truth. In the process the conviction has deepened, and it has served as an anchor, seeing me through life with its varying moods and phases.

51

My mother had been paralyzed for more than two years. One night I had this dream: One evening my mother tells me, "I am tired of lying down, let us go for a walk." I help her out of the bed and out of the room. We begin walking around the house, in the courtyard. When we have walked two sides of the house, she loses the piece of cloth she has around her waist. I tell her that I will bring it back to her, but she says, "Let us carry on, leave the cloth alone." We go on walking. Then I see my sister-in-law and her daughter coming, carrying water. They are laughing, and I tell mother again that I will bring her cloth back to her. She says, "Let them laugh, that does not affect us." We go on walking.

Working through this dream with Tony's guidance I became aware how paralyzed I had been for years—paralyzed by belief systems, doctrines, shoulds and oughts, my need to please others, my fear of what others would think, do, etc. When I "saw" this I was freed. Life has not been the same for me.

52

Tony and I had met on several occasions. One lovely evening we were out walking. We spoke of how our theological views had changed over the years. I admitted quite openly that I had finally ceased believing in a God who could punish, reject, embarrass, or abandon his people ever since I had accepted that God's love was unconditional. I mentioned further that I no longer believed in limbo, judgment, hell, and purgatory—all the things that used to intimidate me about God and religion.

Tony, unfazed, neither agreeing nor disagreeing, said, "Do you still believe in heaven?"

That was all I needed. For many days afterward I reflected. I had another illusion shattered. I realized if I stopped believing in a God of punishment I would logically need to let go of a God of reward. I pondered again, "Who is this God beyond our concepts and projections, who is mystery and love?"

It is so difficult to let God be God, and to simply accept God as mystery for all generations. I realized once again that theology is not spirituality; that concepts passed on by others are not what truth is in reality.

Tony had an uncanny ability to help people drop illusions. I am still being helped.

53

One day I felt down, confused with so much religious teachings and doctrines, etc. Talking to Tony I told him that I didn't seem to believe in anything anymore. He laughed aloud as if I had told him a joke or something. "Who told you to believe?" he asked me. I was taken aback. And suddenly I realized how angry I was with all those who had forced me to believe. I realized I didn't want to continue believing just because others had told me.

All the time Tony pushed us to take responsibility for our actions, for our life. We often reacted to this and tried directly or indirectly to get Tony to tell us which way to take, which choice to make, e.g., about daily Eucharist, our relationships, physical intimacy in our friendships, the form and duration of our prayer, etc. Tony consistently refused to let us hide behind him or his authority and so shirk responsibility. He would give guidelines, but never even implicitly decide for us.

SON: *Dad, how soon will I be old enough to do as I please?*

FATHER: *I don't know. Nobody has lived that long yet.*

54

One day in 1986 Tony and I were walking along the causeway of Lonavla Lake. It was my last meeting with him. The conversation turned to the topic of God. I spoke of my personal experience of God as Father, a loving Father, who meant so much in my life. Tony listened. At a certain moment he said, "When are you going to let go of God, your God? You are using him as crutch, and you won't grow. Your life and your world will be of the crutches. Throw him out and see what happens."

Throw him out. Fall back on my inner resources. Fall back on the God who is in me? Do away with the religious practices which I do out of habit? Stop turning to the Bible and the catechism books for norms of conduct? Listen to the Spirit speaking within me? Test the memorized doctrines on the anvil of reason and experience? Trust myself into the hands of the Mystery which works mightily in the universe? . . .

"One day you may say," Tony said, "I found God, I know him, he is so and so, he is there and there, he is in me, in creation, in the Eucharist. . . . That is a day of disaster for you because you will have found your God, your own projection, so pitiful and small. These gods—these idols—in turn keep us pitiful and small. We would fight for them. It is frightening to hear people talk and threaten with things they only 'believe.' They can be terrible. . . . Mystery does not require defenders. Idols do. Mystery makes us humble."

I have experienced the anxiety and the dangers and the rewards of throwing away crutches.

Pity the poor atheist who feels grateful but has no one to thank.

55

In 1981 during an eight-day retreat to Jesuits preached by Tony, an intense Jesuit seminarian inquired, "I realize that you have been saying quite clearly that everything we do can be a prayer; but how long should a Jesuit pray?" Tony was quiet, but smiled knowingly. The man persisted, "Will you give me an answer?" Tony responded seriously, "How long do you like to pray?" The Jesuit fell silent—unwilling to answer, unable to answer. We never found out.

56

Though I personally have not done Sadhana or any course under Tony, I am a great admirer of him who was a seeker after deeper truth. What I have received from him is the challenging example of a Jesuit who daringly looked into the phony mythologies of religion as it is lived and had the courage to say aloud, that "the emperor has no clothes." He said it with such consummate skill that he effortlessly survived the criticism of many whom his insights disturbed and who thought that he was a danger to orthodox religious life, which of course he probably was.

I cannot honestly say that I have been very deeply "influenced" by Tony in my personal spiritual search and formation. But in the earlier stages of my quest for a meaningful spirituality and humanity for myself, Tony was an inspiring example to me to do my own search without fear and without relying too much on other people to guide me.

57

One weekend, Mario, friend of Tony and housekeeper of Sadhana, gave me the only antique key of an antique room. "I cannot get a duplicate, so don't lose it," he advised. I disappeared into the fields. While watching the sunbirds do their provocative sun dance in the sunset, I slipped into my "cloud of unknowing" and woke much later, to find my key was spirited away. I looked in the canal, near where I rested, behind every bush. It was nowhere. I went back to the kitchen to tell Mario. He was annoyed. After Mario left, I prayed to Saint Anthony, the saint of lost and found things.

Just then Anthony de Mello appeared and asked, "Where's Mario?" I responded, "Why?" He looked silly and said, "I lost my room key. Only Mario can help me get into my room." I nearly fell out of the window. I exclaimed, "You too! Were you roaming in the gloaming like me?" He looked surprised, "Why, have you lost your key too?" "Of course I have," I replied, "then that makes two of us. I don't feel so bad now." Tony disappeared into his Sadhana wilderness.

Next morning at breakfast I said, "Tony, I have a hunch that you made that story up about the lost key, only to make me feel good! True?" He laughed and said, "Now suppose I made it up, would it make you feel different? And suppose it was true, would you feel bad? What matters is that you feel good!" That was the sage speaking: like all his stories and himself, lovingly detached. No such thing as good luck or bad luck. What is, is.

58

During the renewal in 1982 the group had decided to go to Ajanta-Ellora. I was much excited about it. Two days before the excursion Tony quietly came to me and asked me, "Could you do me a favor?" Certainly, but what favor could I do him? He put some money in my pocket and said, "You take this. You may need it for the excursion. And do not tell anyone."

One day I went to Tony's room in Lonavla and asked reluctantly if he could give me a refill for my dot-pen. He was sitting and writing something. He turned around and said with a serious face: "Are you, Rita, asking me, Tony, your friend, for a refill. . . !" I was confused for a second. Then Tony held out to me a beautiful pen!

I felt ashamed of myself for having been so reluctant to ask him. I became aware of my own stinginess.

I was in Sadhana for a few days mainly to spend time with a friend. One evening Tony called me to his room and putting 300 rupees in my hand he said, "Michael, I don't think your province will have given you much money. Take this, take your friend out for a good dinner, and enjoy your days here."

My brother was terminally ill. Tony sent some money to me with a note: "Mathew, my prayers for your brother and you."

Tony told us in the group this little experience. He was going abroad, and a young Jesuit asked him to bring a good foreign basketball. Tony was not enthusiastic about the errand and actually felt silly when he met the young man in question and produced the ball he had somehow managed to bring along. "On seeing the ball," Tony said, "that young man's face suddenly lit up so brightly, he expressed such delight, and jumped for sheer joy, that all the troubles in bringing the ball were forgotten." Tony drew the conclusion that a gift need not be repaid with a return gift; the very joy of receiving it is its best recompense. I recalled a statement of Karl Barth: "Joy is the most eloquent way to show gratitude."

59

It happened in the early part of 1980. A morning group therapy session. My problem: for some time now I feel a growing dislike of groups, of crowds, as if something is pulling me away from them; a growing attraction also for silence and solitude which is not usual for me; a strong pull for an ashram type of life. . . .

Tony knew me from previous contacts. Looking at me he asked a few questions and guided me through a fantasy that made me go back to Manipur, my community there, my work with the students and the different situations I now had left behind. Emotions connected with those years and events welled up in me, yet I controlled myself. Tony asked me to go outside, be by myself, take as much time as I needed and go over the whole situation once again allowing my feelings freely to flow. I did. Returning after one and a half hours, I told him that I was happy to go over that part of my life once again, but that to my surprise I did not cry much. He did not seem to mind.

Then he said,

> You are thinking that losing Manipur, your favorite place, you have lost everything beautiful in life. You feel there cannot be anything beautiful and wonderful in life any-more . . . so you are trying to withdraw from life. No. Think of the persons and places, the experiences and the kind of life lived in your heaven. For each of these, be grateful . . . and say good-bye to them. Take your time, go through each of your experiences and say good-bye. Remember, new things are waiting for you, new places, new experiences, new people, new challenges. . . .

You have to die in order to live. This is resurrection: to say good-bye, to let go, to move on. Only then can you live fully.

To be fully alive is to live in the present. To live in the present is to live in the presence. When you are in Kerala, be there with your whole being. Now in Lonavla, be fully here. Your heart is still in Manipur while your body is here. You want to solve the problem by withdrawing into an ashram. No. Be where you are—fully. Life is not yesterday. Life is not tomorrow. Life is now. So is love. So is God. Live in the present to experience life as it is now, for eternal life is now: eternal life is here.

During the Eucharist later that day, using the theme of dying and living, Tony commented on the joy of saying good-bye. I came to see the meaning of the Resurrection in a new light.

No, I did not go to the ashram. Having learned to shed the burden of the past, I enjoy a new freedom to live fully where I am working now.

60

"All appreciation and love are not only unnecessary, they are a hindrance." This was Tony's provocative opening statement of a session of the 1986 Sadhana renewal.

> Getting the taste of praise and appreciation we will start needing it, an artificial acquired need, an invention of human society. It is a "world-need," not a "soul-need." Having got the taste of that appreciation and love we will manipulate to get it, be unhappy and depressed when we don't get it, prostitute ourselves for it, make comparisons in the light of it, and use it for gaining power and position.
>
> We need less of "world-emotion" and more of "soul-emotion" like enjoying nature, intimacy, watching a sunset, laughter, the enjoyment of the sense pleasures which do not come from compulsion, compensation, etc. . . .

61

Through different sessions I was helped to become more and more aware of myself, identify my feelings of jealousy and ambition, the hidden agendas and the games I play.

To a great extent I was able to make objective decisions, to adopt healthy feelings and behavioral patterns. Whenever I did this I felt a space within me—a feeling of liberation. Subsequently I became aware of my feeling of pride and a feeling of superiority. Then I began to question myself: "What difference does it make to get rid of a negative feeling and then feel proud about the same?"

Tony's answer to this was in the form of a story. "The disciple asked the Master, 'What did you get by enlightenment?' The Master said, 'Before enlightenment I used to be depressed; after enlightenment I continue to be depressed. But there is a great difference. Before the enlightenment the depression made me unhappy, and after the enlightenment the depression comes and goes without upsetting me—just like the cloud over the sky which comes and goes.'"

Watch the pride come and go. Today it is pride, tomorrow something else. Watch them come and go. Be aware.

Similarly, in discernment, so often we seek after God's will in obscurity, clouded by our emotions and prejudices. Watch them come and go. In the transparency that follows, one will be able to discern freely.

MOTHER: *Your face is clean, but how did you get your hands so dirty?*

SON: *Washing my face.*

62

There was a time when I was a very critical person. While I was telling Tony of my indignation at the behavior of some of my confreres, he gently challenged me to look into myself and find out why I was so indignant and critical. What is it in me that prevents me from seeing human beings as lovable notwithstanding what I regard in them as unbecoming? What blinds my heart to the reality that a few mistakes do not make them any less worthy of love, just as my weaknesses and mistakes have not made me less worthy of love in the eyes of my friends?

It had struck me how after Tony's death so many said that they had felt personally loved by him.

The Bible tells us to love our neighbors and also to love our enemies, probably because they are generally the same people.

63

I have a tendency to react to people, to feel "challenged," and this affects adversely my communication with people. A piece of advice from Tony, simple as it was, has proved very helpful to me during my six years in office as provincial: "Don't see every challenge to your authority leveled by a subject who comes to you as an act of disobedience, or as an attack on your authority or person. Rather see it as a possible problem of the person, which often it is."

And on another occasion Tony said, "We often mix up statements which persons make to us with their relationship to us. Then we get hooked in our insecurity, etc. . . . and we feel the statement as a judgment or a 'challenge,' as being put down, humiliating. . . ."

64

One day during a retreat, when talking with co-retreatants, we got stuck with what we felt was a contradiction in the life of Jesus. How could he who had said "Do not be anxious: look at the lilies in the field and the birds in the air . . . they are not anxious about tomorrow. . . ," how could he be so depressed and anxious before he died? He was not practicing what he preached!

Pointing out that we terribly mixed up piety and spirituality, Tony said, "Many of our difficulties, emotions—positive and negative—are the result of our conditioning. To be spiritual means that we understand that we are not those depressions, we are not those anxieties. To be spiritual does not mean not to have anxieties or depressions but to lovingly accept anything that comes our way." He went on to say:

> Let us suppose a person has a severe inferiority complex. Whatever you do, he will get all upset, irritated, and so on. Now is it possible for this person to get enlightened, to attain spirituality? Of course it is. He could still have all his psychological hang-ups and be very spiritual, if he understands his complex and his fears and upsets as something like the clouds.
>
> To see Jesus as "above" all anxieties as you would have him before his death, is piety, a plastic Jesus. It is a superficial understanding of Jesus and of what he is saying. Not to be anxious about tomorrow is to attain a state where whether you are anxious or not, you can accept everything.
>
> Now this cannot be produced. This comes from understanding something, from seeing something.

These insights have helped me to keep my balance, not to be moody or upset for a long time, to dissociate the events from myself, especially when I was in authority. It made me realize how often people react not really against me, but against the particular role I happened to have at that time. It made a difference in my life and now looking back at those years, not easy years by any means, I realize how being spiritual in the sense Tony meant has helped me very much.

65

I received counseling in one group session in Sadhana and at the end of it I felt on top of the world. But a few days later I was back to square one: feeling jealous, anxious. In addition to all that, I was now ashamed before the group for the relapse. With much inner struggle I talked about this in the group. Tony asked, "The other day Paul revealed so much of his own weaknesses before the group; did you lose your esteem for him?" "No, on the contrary, it had risen." "Then why do you think you will lose affection, esteem, etc. . . . for revealing your weakness?"

That set me reflecting: Am I not projecting my own feelings onto the others, my own ways? Can I love myself with my so-called weaknesses? Can I love others with their weaknesses? Cannot a person criticize me without ceasing to love me? Cannot one be angry without losing affection? . . . I was learning the first lessons of loving myself and others as each one is.

Another response from Tony a few days later which had a lasting effect on me also comes to mind. "You are worried that what you said the other day might have been misunderstood by some. You want to explain and clear the misunderstanding. Later on when you are doing bigger jobs and dealing with people from different places, surely many will misunderstand you. To clear all these misunderstandings you will have to be constantly traveling up and down the country. . . . John, what does it matter that some people misunderstand you? *What . . . does . . . it . . . matter. . . ?*"

In 1987 I told Tony about some hurts, humiliations, etc. . . . I had suffered in recent months.

His response was something like the following: "Who is this *I* you are speaking of, an *I* who can get hurt, humiliated, etc. . . ? Is it your body? Is it your mind, or your soul? Surely the mind or the soul cannot get hurt, humiliated by what someone said or did. So what is getting hurt, etc. . . . is an *I* you posit. You are accustomed to think there is an *I*. You are conditioned to think certain things affect the *I*. It is a figment of your imagination. It is a creation of society. Liberation comes when you know there is no *I* to get hurt or loved or appreciated or rejected. *I* as a subject of 'good' and 'bad' experiences is a myth which has become deeply rooted in our psyche."

I did not understand. I do not understand it even now. I have a feeling there is more to this topic than Tony saw. Anyway this could be said, as indeed some reviewers have done: Tony had a profound experience of transcending the self, and it is that experience he is exploring and communicating in these puzzling statements about the *I* and the *self*.

The idea that there really is no *I* to get affected positively or negatively, to be worried about, continues to intrigue me.

TEACHER: *What's the difference between a porpoise and a dolphin?*

STUDENT: *That's what I say, what's the difference?*

66

I cherished my weekly walks with Tony to Lonavla Lake during my maxi-Sadhana days. Walking toward the lake we would invariably take our places on the parapet of the bridge and in absolute silence, facing the western sky beyond the lake, we would watch the sunset. No, not watch it, but take it in. . . . "Do not verbalize the scene, Geeta, just watch and let the colors come and go," Tony would say. Taking in the colors, the deepening shadows on the lake, the changing hues . . . time stood still.

"When I look at the horizon," Tony said on a particular occasion, his eyes fixed on the distant scene, "I think of creation. Time touches eternity. I wonder how many millions of sunsets this spot has witnessed. I think of the life force of countless people who have watched the sunsets before us and of the millions who will do so after us. You and I are two insignificant yet infinitely precious particles in the heart of the universe that throbs with the Heart of Christ. If people were to look at the infinity of space and allow their hearts to be in tune with the Universal Soul, they would stop their savage hunt for power and wealth."

"The life force of the millions who have gone before us . . . in tune with the Universal soul. . . ." Was it a pagan concept, I thought for a while with uneasiness. Yet, these concepts and that evening on the bank of the lake have awakened a deep yearning in me to live my life to the fullest, knowing there is so much more to space and time than what our eyes perceive.

More, however, was to come. It was one Saturday, again on our weekly walk. As we were nearing the lake Tony suddenly stood still. As he resumed walking he spoke to me of death and detachment and pain, ideas he had been grappling with on those days. At that quiet moment he "saw" clearly that attachment to anyone or anything brought with it pain and unfreedom. He was deeply loyal to his friends, a few of whom he loved very deeply. Yet on this occasion he said, "I am held to my friends by a tiny thread. The whole of me yearns to cut off that one strand that holds me back from flying. The whole of me yearns for that exhilarating sense of freedom. Yet part of me enjoys the crawling." This was the time when he wrote those meditations which were published posthumously, under the title *Called to Love.*

That very day after watching the sunset we walked some distance in silence, my heart full of forebodings. Standing still at the end of the bridge Tony said, "I see the new Sadhana building as my mausoleum. I know I will not live in it for long. I see it clearly. My life is coming to an end." I was frightened by his words. I could not think of losing him. Yet my heart sensed that I too had to let go if I loved him.

A year later when I received news of his death, the memory of that evening stood out. And I knew his greatest gift to me was the sunset.

67

I had sent Tony a copy of my article in which I suggested that prayer is not for getting anything from God, not an obligation. It is an end in itself, as it is an expression of love, best done in silence. After reading it he wrote, "Well, last night I certainly sat down and read your article at leisure. I found it most interesting and even daring. However, as you have frequently told me in the past, it is not possible to put the whole truth into print. I have myself come to a position that all prayer (as we traditionally understand the word) is a pure waste of time. It merely caters to the fantasy needs of the people who have a compulsion to placate a deity. What a tragedy to see so many hours wasted in worship that could have been spent in reading a good book and, even better, in advancing in self-understanding and self-knowledge. Now that I say this I must add that I have become much more radical in my thinking and much more daring—perhaps even rash—in the way I speak. I will be giving a prayer seminar in Pune at the end of April 1987 in which I plan to change my whole mode of presentation and also a good deal of the subject matter. I have stopped calling them *prayer seminars,* and I call them *spirituality courses.* So life keeps interesting because I continue to keep changing."

68

I had many occasions to spend some quiet moments with Tony. The most memorable was the two days I spent with him in Sadhana on our way back from the last seminar that he gave in Pune. That was one week before he died. There are many things that he said then which I recall now. I have applied these to my very troubled life in the past few months and have found them to be very effective, and they have brought me much peace and happiness.

1. A grateful heart can never be unhappy.

2. Everyday when you wake up remind yourself that you may not see tomorrow. If you do this you will enjoy each day.

3. Think of death and you will start to live. We never think of death; so we cling to things and persons, and end up leading a miserable life, afraid that we may lose them.

4. Don't get attached to things in life, enjoy them while they are there, remember one day you have to leave them behind, you cannot take them with you. Is it worth all the misery we go through trying to keep them?

5. One thing he said that day stands out very clearly in my memory: "If I die tomorrow and I knew I was going to die, the thing that would make me very happy is that I have helped so many people. My being on this earth has been of some use to humankind." How many people are able to say this of their life on this earth? Do we spend our time doing things for ourselves or helping others?

6. We always have everything we need to be happy. It is what we want and cannot have that we concentrate on and we are therefore miserable.

69

It was difficult for me to face angry and rude people. I could not stand their shouting.

I had told this to Tony earlier, and he had given me different exercises which helped me in a small way. Yet I used to get sort of paralyzed in those situations. Then on one occasion instead of giving me an exercise, he chose to give me the following explanation:

> Whenever you encounter a troublesome person, do not identify her as cruel, stupid, etc. Instead, see her as a frightened person. This is exactly what the cruel or rude person is. All negative emotions have a foundation in fear. Her angry aggressiveness is the only method she presently knows for releasing her tension or fear.
>
> If you take the wrong view of seeing her as cruel or hateful, this will have a definite effect on the way you try to deal with her. It makes you afraid of her, for negativity in one person arouses negativity in another. So if you turn negatively to this person you cannot deal with her wisely and tactfully.
>
> See what happens when you understand. The process is reversed. Instead of her negativity transferring itself to you, you transfer your positiveness to her. Try this miracle method for yourself in a specific situation. It is remarkable what changes it makes.

On another occasion when I asked Tony how I could protect myself from the cruelty of other persons, from someone hurting me or being cruel to me, he answered me in the same vein: through understanding.

70

Tony led me to seek counsel and strength above all in myself. "When you see clearly that a position you have adopted, a judgment you have made is clean, uninfluenced by the ego, then you will have also the strength to act accordingly."

He wrote to me once: "At the moment you don't experience the strength because you don't see yourself clearly. Truth will make you free. Knowing yourself as you are without the admixture of lies you will become steady. And then you can stand up to anything, anyone."

Going deep into myself I began to discover what I was doing with myself: my dishonest ways of dealing with my thoughts and feelings, my difficulty in accepting the positive and negative remarks about me. . . . Through this continued honest awareness I began to enjoy greater freedom and serenity when facing adverse situations and in this Tony offered me a warm understanding along with a loving and affectionate challenge.

71

During the last years of his life a rapid change was happening in Tony. As I was relating with him very closely I could see this transformation clearly. He used to write to me in detail about his insights and experiences. "I feel as if I am forced to follow this new path from within, as if I am urged strongly to live only in the present," he once mentioned to me. It led him to decisions which were painful, no doubt, yet I understood him and never doubted his love for me.

On one occasion I asked him, "Is there a place for emotions in your new way of thinking?" "Yes, of course there is, my dear," he answered, "otherwise life would be so dull. But there is no place for negative emotions—all that kind of suffering is really a waste of time and a waste of precious life. Negative emotions always come from our wrong perceptions and wrong ideas. But for positive emotions there is plenty of place—however, positive emotions that are aroused by present reality, not by past memories, because to return to the past is to return to what is dead."

Yes, I understood him and loved him even more: loving without clinging. It has been a powerful experience in my life.

72

In one of the last sessions of my maxi-Sadhana Tony repeated an idea he had mentioned earlier: "If you do not make progress, it will not be because you lack goodwill but because you lack memory. . . . Don't bank on any 'breakthrough' you have had. Their benefits will gradually vanish unless you remember to strengthen them through daily practice. Your neurotic patterns will be with you tomorrow also. You will have slumps. Then recall what you had understood about them and how you had come out of them. Keep practicing the new patterns, the new responses, the fantasies and exercises which have helped you. In the course of time the old habit's grip on you might ease. In any case you will not be the same—if you remember to keep up the practice every day.

"You will be like the man who mentioned to his community a few months after his Sadhana course: 'I still get into fixes a lot of times, but I laugh more and certainly am a lot more at peace.' Or," Tony added mischievously, "like the man who wet his pants when confronted by his boss. The considerate boss sent him to a urologist who sent him to a psychologist. 'Did the psychologist help you?' 'Yes, I used to feel bad about the affair, now I don't anymore!'"

A tramp knocked at a farmer's door and asked for some food.

"Are you a Christian?" asked the farmer.

"Of course," said the tramp. "Can't you tell? Just look at the knees of my pants. Don't they prove it?"

The farmer and his wife noticed the holes in the knees and promptly gave the man some food.

As the tramp turned to go, the farmer asked, "By the way, what made those holes in the seat of your pants?"

"Backsliding," said the tramp.

"... SO HAPPY, SO FREE...."

Bombay, the early seventies. Tony is spiritual guide of the young Jesuit seminarians. We had to rush him to the hospital. He had acute pain in the kidney region. Doctors found him dehydrated. He had been experimenting with fasting. For nearly a week he had not taken food or water. After his recovery Tony told me: "You may fast of food but never of water. The system needs to be flushed." Tony had learned from experience and this was important to him.

Tony had been to Spain for the study of philosophy. There he met a Jesuit, Father Calveras, who held even in those pre-Vatican days that "The prayer of the Jesuits has become too speculative. Ignatius has given great importance to the emotions in prayer." Tony was deeply impressed when Calveras asked him, "How do you pray? Describe the way you pray." Tony thought, "Here is a true guru." The spiritual guide awakened in him.

I remember him telling me once: "I thought of experimenting with drugs under a doctor's supervision." He wanted to know from within so as to be able to speak from experience in guiding others. To the best of my knowledge he never experimented with drugs.

It was characteristic of Tony to want to share what he had. He derived pleasure in doing so. Tony would have mischievously asked, "Did I consent to the pleasure?" Well, since he always was in a journey of discovery he had plenty to share—books, experiences, anecdotes, ideas. . . . He applied his mind and heart to his discoveries, researched them, experimented with them, probed into them . . . finally he would discard much of it and integrate some. Then he would enrich others with his findings.

Tony was reading the life of Swami Ramdas. He was fascinated by the man. He shared his findings with the junior scholastics. Tony stressed that men like Swami Ramdas were Indian saints worthy of imitation. The juniors were taken up with Swami Ramdas. As a starter they wanted to imitate him in his way of dressing. In a few days they started parading themselves in *dhoties* and *sadras*. When some of the community raised their eyebrows, Tony explained with aplomb: "Young people need to express their creativity; better they do it in a constructive 'fashion.' Would you prefer them to wear jeans and T-shirts and sing pop-music?"

Tony knew how to sell his goods, and he was aware of it. I heard him say more than once, "I can be dangerous. Because of my persuasiveness I can convince the devil himself."

Once on our way back from a walk Tony told me that his dream was to do something for the education of the poor children. He wanted to raise a fund in Sadhana for this purpose. That day he added that it was time for him to hand over Sadhana to someone.

I asked Tony if he was not proud of the new Sadhana building coming up and the money he collected through his books and talks. He laughed loudly and said: "I got some grey matter upstairs and I do bla-bla-bla . . . and collect some money. If you had it, you would also do bla-bla-bla . . . and collect some money and so what is there to be proud of. It is not mine."

One evening I went out for a walk with Tony. We were discussing freedom and happiness. Suddenly Tony stood still, silent. After a few seconds he told me: "How I wish I could show you what I see. You will have to find it yourself." After that we walked on and continued with our discussion.

One day in 1985 during a prayer seminar Tony was at pains to convey that "We cannot know God. The moment you give a flower a name, you lose the reality: the moment you give God a name, you lose God." To this, one participant said bluntly, "Tony, you know nothing of metaphysics." He let it pass. Afterward he told me, "I felt hurt by that remark. Many think I will not feel it. I do, and I want to remain open to feeling hurt."

I appreciated Tony greatly as I considered him an extraordinary person. When I try to recall my encounters with him, I am surprised to know that they were mostly negative. I did not like the way he avoided disagreement and confrontation by countering with an ad hominem retort or attack. I was the victim of this repeatedly. Such experiences hurt me and confused me about him and distanced me somewhat from him emotionally.

Tony said to me, "I gave myself fully to preaching retreats. Then I saw 95 percent of the religious are not ready for the retreats, hindered as they are by psychological problems. So I started Sadhana, and now I am fully in that period." Then with a sparkle in his eyes he added: "What will be next? I don't know. Maybe I'll marry. . . ."

Tony once told me personally: "If I had to do it over again, I would not have written the book *Sadhana*." That would have been a matter of weeks before he died. His most translated book, and he regretted having written it. I'm not sure why.

I heard Tony say several times what he had said before four hundred people in Spain: "I do not any more stand by my first book, *Sadhana,* and it does not represent my present thinking. I allow it to be reprinted because my publishers want it."

In 1977 Tony had told us conscious breathing called *anna-panna* was the only kind of prayer he had now used for a long time. He gave the following instance: "The other day I became a frightened child, without peace and without relief, and my instinct led me to go out to the garden and concentrate on my breathing. Soon I returned to my own quieted self."

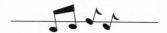

I never saw Tony weak. I was afraid of him, and I sometimes felt a disgust for him especially when he laughed loud. I kept my distance from him. I don't think I was ready to meet him man to man. In his letters he was inviting; face to face I found he was rejecting. I felt envious of a couple of his favorites. My last encounter with Tony was not a pleasant one. I felt rejected by him. He was fed up of me being childish and feeling helpless.

Once as we were coming out of the Sadhana building to go for an evening walk, Tony said, "Something is happening to me. I am doing a lot of things. I am not planning to do them. They are done by me and through me."

He wrote on March 14, 1985: "I have not been too well of late—I suspect it was connected with my blood pressure which I had been neglecting recently. Well, I suppose I have to learn the lesson that as the years go by I am not getting any younger!"

From a letter in early 1986:

. . . there are so many things I want to write about, but something has happened to me today and I just cannot write. Last night I had a horrible experience—one of the worst experiences of my life—and I could not sleep much. It would take too long to describe, but it was a kind of feeling of despair and fright and a terrible loneliness. . . . as if nobody could reach me, no one could touch me, I was just abandoned by God and everyone. And I woke up with such a fright, sweating in spite of the intense cold, so I had to open the windows and walk up and down the room. If that despair had lasted longer I felt I would go mad. This morning I talked with someone about it. I feel it is some kind of spiritual experience. . . . The whole of today I have been feeling a kind of sadness and very tired and I was forcing myself to do the essential task that had to be done. . . . N. B., please don't worry about my sadness—twice before I have had this kind of sadness . . . and I have gradually grown out of it."

From a letter of March 2, 1986: ". . . Why have I been feeling physically exhausted? Because of a strange phenomenon that has come into my life: the meditations. These days I am going through strange spiritual movements and I feel a compulsion to put them down in the form of meditations and give them to the group. I just cannot resist this compulsion and sometimes I spend as much as three hours a day composing one meditation. . . ."

From a letter of March 8, 1986: "There is one thing I love more than you. And that thing I love more than myself. In comparison with that we are nothing, I am nothing—like pale candle light flames compared to the sun."

When I met Tony for the last time in March 1987, shortly before the last Sadhana renewal at Lonavla, I had the feeling that he had removed all the cover in his way of speaking, and I felt that he would be silenced by Rome. He said he did not care anymore. Whether he spoke or not, it mattered little to him. He was ready for anything.

From a letter of April 14, 1987: "If things had been all right I would have come to. . . . And yet I am perfectly peaceful and content to be here in the cool of the morning, gazing out of the window at the serenity of the scenery . . . the bright sunshine, the cool breeze, the young leaves sprouting in the trees and the clear blue sky. Everything is so soaked in peacefulness and life. That is the way our hearts should be as we go through life. I can sense that my heart is moving toward this, though there are so many mountain loads of rubbish and illusions to remove. I am happier than ever before in my life."

From the same letter of April 14, 1987: ". . . I am quite amazed that in spite of the work entailed by the renewal, I am not tired at all. I feel some kind of a congestion in the chest. I wonder if that is what they call a chest cold. Anyway, except for that, I feel perfectly fit."

On April 29, 1987, a few weeks before he died he answered my request to meet him after his return from the United States: "I don't know when or where we will meet; perhaps you will see me next, sitting under a bodhi tree naked and silent!"

From Tony's last letter of June 1, 1987, the day before he died: ". . . I find the whole of my interest is now focused on something else, on the 'world of the Spirit,' and I see everything else as trifling and so irrelevant . . . never before in my life have I felt so happy, so free. . . ."